Contents

Each page has a title telling you what it is about.

Time

T2.2

1 Write these units of time in order, from smallest to largest.

hour   day   month   year

second   minute   fortnight   week

Instructions look like this. Always read these carefully before starting.

Write the units of time that are:

2 less than an hour

3 more than a month

4 the same as 2 weeks

5 less than a week

6 more than a minute, but less than a day

7 more than a week, but less than a year.

2. minute, ...

This shows how to set out your work.

Write the units you would use to measure how long:

8 a runner takes to run a marathon (26 miles)

9 a football match takes

10 a holiday at the seaside might last

11 a large meal takes to eat

12 your granny has lived

13 a baby less than 2 years old has lived

14 it takes to climb a tree

15 your favourite television programme lasts.

Think of something that takes about:
a) 6 hours b) 6 months.

These are Rocket activities. Ask your teacher if you need to do these questions.

Read this to check you understand what you have been learning on the page.

I can understand and use appropriate units of time

Calendars

1 List the months in each season. Write the months of the year in order.

April   December   August   November   September   May

June   October   January   February   July   March

WINTER   SPRING   SUMMER   AUTUMN

Look at Chang's calendar for **June**, then answer the questions.

June						
Monday	Tuesday	Wednesday	Thursday	Friday	Saturday	Sunday
1	2	3	4	5	6	7
8	9	10	11	12	13	14

On what date did Chang go:

2 swimming   **3** camping   **4** to Aunt Su's house

5 horse riding   **6** to his trumpet lesson   **7** to band practice?

Draw a calendar for what you will do this week.

I can work with dates and months of the year

3

Calendars

Study Jim's calender, then answer the questions.

September						
Monday	**Tuesday**	**Wednesday**	**Thursday**	**Friday**	**Saturday**	**Sunday**
1 Washing day	2	3 Dad to go back to Navy	4	5	6 Aunt May for lunch	7
8 Washing day	9	10	11	12 Rally at town hall	13	14 Aunt May for lunch
15 Washing day	16 Post Gran's present	17	18	19 Gran's birthday	20	21
22 Washing day	23	24 Help with harvest	25 Help with harvest	26 Help with harvest	27 Help with harvest	28 Harvest festival
29 Washing day	30					

1 How many Tuesdays were there in September?

2 Which days were the washing days?

3 On which date did Dad return to the Navy?

4 How many days was Jim helping with the harvest?

5 How many times did Aunt May come to lunch? What were the dates?

6 How many days were there between posting Gran's present and her birthday?

7 When was the rally?

Talk with your partner about how your month's calendar might be different.

I can work with calendars

Time

1 Write these units of time in order, from smallest to largest.

hour   day   month   year

second   minute   fortnight   week

2. minute, ...

Write the units of time that are:

2 less than an hour

3 more than a month

4 the same as 2 weeks

5 less than a week

6 more than a minute, but less than a day

7 more than a week, but less than a year.

Write the units you would use to measure how long:

8 a runner takes to run a marathon (26 miles)

9 a football match takes

10 a holiday at the seaside might last

11 a large meal takes to eat

12 your granny has lived

13 a baby less than 2 years old has lived

14 it takes to climb a tree

15 your favourite television programme lasts.

Think of something that takes about:
a) 6 hours b) 6 months.

Time

Write each time as am or pm.

`1. 4:00 pm`

1   four o'clock in the afternoon

2   ten to one in the morning

3   half past six in the evening

4   twenty past midnight

5   six o'clock in the morning

6   half past ten at night

7   quarter to eight in the morning

8   twenty-five past two in the afternoon

9   five to six in the afternoon

10 quarter past three in the afternoon

Write each as a digital time, using a 24 hour clock.

`11. 00:14`

11

am

12

pm

13

am

14

pm

15

am

16

pm

Write some 24 hour times where the hours and the minutes are the same, e.g. 16:16. Mark each one as am or pm.

I can use am and pm times and write them as 24 hour times

Time

Write each time using a 24 hour clock.

1. 9:05

1. five past seven pm
2. two-fifteen am
3. six forty-two pm
4. eight-thirteen am
5. quarter to seven am
6. twenty-five past eight pm
7. nine fifty-three am
8. twelve past three pm
9. half past four pm
10. five thirty-five am

True or false?

11. Ten minutes after midnight is 12:10 on a 24 hour clock.

12. Twenty to four can be 15:40 or 03:40.

13. 13:13 is around lunchtime.

14. From 10:30 to 14:00 is $4\frac{1}{2}$ hours.

15. 17:30 is midway between 10 am and midnight.

16. An hour later than ten to five in the morning is 05:50.

How many palindromic digital times can you write, e.g. 15:51?
How many are am times and how many are pm times?

I can write 24 hour times

Time problems

Solve these problems.

1   Josh turned on the TV at 4:26 pm and turned it off at 5:00 pm. How many minutes was the TV on for?

2   A film started at 7:02 pm and finished at 8:56 pm. Exactly how long was the film?

3   Cartoons started at 4:50 pm and were on for 30 minutes. When did they end?

4   The news began at 6:05 pm and finished at 6:51 pm. How many minutes was it on for?

5   The football match on TV lasted for 90 minutes and there was a 15 minute break at half-time. It began at 7:45 pm. What time did it finish?

6   Tonight's film begins at 9:00 pm and ends at 10:15 pm. Tomorrow's film is twice as long. It begins at 9:00 pm. What time does it end?

7   Three episodes of a TV show began at 10:30 am and finished at 11:45 am. How long was each episode if the episodes ran straight on without any gaps?

Make up three time problems of your own for your partner to solve.

I can solve time problems and calculate time differences

Time problems

A taxi driver has a busy day.

I.3 8 minutes

> I picked up a man at 4:27 pm and dropped him at his home at 5:05 pm.

I How long was this journey?

> I picked up a woman at 6:48 am and dropped her off at work 30 minutes later.

2 What time did the woman arrive at work?

> The journey from the station to the town centre usually takes 26 minutes. Today it took I hour and II minutes.

3 How much longer was this trip than usual?

> Each weekday I pick up a man at 7:56 am and drop him at work at 8:26 am.

4 How many hours each week does the taxi driver drive this man?

> I left home and drove for 35 minutes to collect Mrs Clark. I arrived there at 12:07 pm.

5 What time did the taxi driver leave home?

> I started driving at 11:25 pm. I took a break at 12:40 am.

6 How long did the taxi driver drive before taking a break?

> Make up three problems like this for your partner to solve.

I can solve time problems and calculate time differences

Time problems

Jo bakes a cake for her gran.

> She goes to the shop to buy the ingredients ($\frac{3}{4}$ hour trip).
> She mixes up the ingredients (10 minutes).
> She and her dad bake the cake in the oven ($\frac{1}{2}$ hour).
> She waits for the cake to cool (55 minutes).

I. 2 hours and 2 0 minutes

1. How long in total did it take from going shopping to when the cake was cool?

2. Jo went to the shops at 12:55 pm. What time did she get home?

3. The cake went into the oven at 13:50. What time did Jo get it out?

4. At what time was the cake cool?

5. At 15:45, Jo decides to put marzipan and icing on the cake. Each layer takes 12 minutes. She puts on a layer of marzipan and two layers of icing. How long does this take altogether?

6. What is the time when she finishes?

7. Her dad takes her to her gran's house at 4:50 pm. How long does Jo have to wait until they leave?

8. The journey to her gran's takes 25 minutes. What time do they arrive?

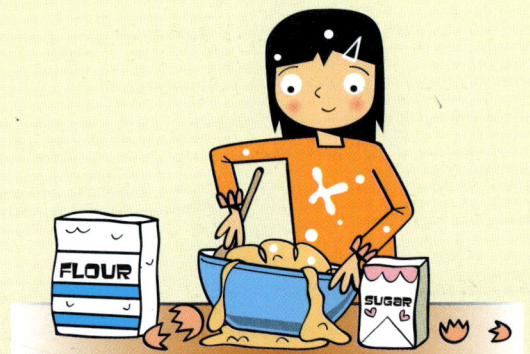

Make up three time problems like this for your partner to solve.

I can solve time problems and calculate time differences

Timetables

1 A train calls at five towns. The timetable has been cut up. Use the information to draw up a single timetable with the times of all the trains.

Dozetown
11:03
12:52
15:31
18:18

Sleepville
10:54
12:43
15:22
18:09

Snoreton
10:15
12:04
14:43
17:30

Little Boring
10:32
12:21
15:00
17:47

Snoozeford
11:26
13:15
15:54
18:41

Write how long it takes to get from:

2. 17 minutes

2 Snoreton to Little Boring

3 Little Boring to Sleepville

4 Sleepville to Dozetown

5 Dozetown to Snoozeford

6 Snoreton to Sleepville

7 Little Boring to Dozetown

8 Sleepville to Snoozeford

9 Little Boring to Snoozeford.

10 How long is the train's total journey?

A train goes from A to B. It takes 2 hours and 45 minutes, and stops in three places. Devise a timetable and calculate the time from each stop to the next.

I can work out time differences from timetables

Timetables

Place		Flight 1	Flight 2	Flight 3
London	take off	10:30	12:30	14:30
Paris	land	11:35	13:35	15:35
	take off	12:05	14:05	16:05
Amsterdam	land	13:40	15:40	17:40
	take off	14:20	16:20	18:20
Dublin	land	15:55	17:55	19:55
	take off	16:25	18:25	20:25
Edinburgh	land	17:05	19:05	21:05
	take off	17:25	19:25	21:25
London	land	18:35	20:35	22:35

Three planes start in London and go to Paris, then Amsterdam, then Dublin, then Edinburgh. Then they go back to London. Look at the timetable and answer these questions.

At what times do planes take off from:

1 Dublin 2 London 3 Paris?

At what times do planes land in:

4 Edinburgh 5 Paris 6 London?

How long are these journeys?

7 Amsterdam to Dublin 8 Paris to Amsterdam
9 London to Paris 10 Dublin to Edinburgh.

Think of four places you would like to visit. Draw up your own plane timetable.

I can work with timetables and answer questions about them

Organising time

1   Chloe has lots to do on Saturday.

Draw a time line to help her plan her day.

|—|—|—|—|—|—|—|—|—|—|
9:00 10:00 11:00 12:00 1:00 2:00 3:00 4:00 5:00 6:00

You will need to decide which things are most important. She might not fit everything in.

Chloe wants to visit her gran. That will take $1\frac{1}{2}$ hours.

Chloe's dad is taking her to a football match which starts at 3 pm. It takes 20 minutes to get there and lasts for 105 minutes.

Chloe has promised to wash her mum's car before 12:00 pm. This will take about 1 hour.

The library is open between 10 am and 2 pm and she wants to take a book back. This would take $\frac{1}{2}$ hour.

Chloe wants to go swimming for an hour. The pool is open between 9 am and 1 pm.

The supermarket is open between 9 am and 5 pm. Chloe must go there for $\frac{1}{2}$ hour.

Chloe will also need to fit in having lunch. That takes about $\frac{1}{2}$ hour.

2   Compare your answers with your partner's.

> Draw your own time line of things you might do during a weekend.

I can organise events and record them on a time line

Organising time

Lachlan has lots of after-school clubs during the week.

	Monday	Tuesday	Wednesday	Thursday	Friday
3:15					
3:30					
3:45					
4:00					
4:15					
4:30					
4:45					
5:00					
5:15					
5:30					
5:45					

I Draw up a timetable to help his mum know what time to collect him each day. Use these statements to help you organise it.

On Wednesdays at 3:30 pm, Lachlan goes to football practice which lasts for I hour I5 minutes.

On Mondays, Lachlan starts a 30 minute trumpet lesson at 3:15 pm.

On Fridays, Lachlan goes to Scouts which lasts for I hour. It finishes at 5 pm.

On Tuesdays at 4:30 pm, Lachlan does gymnastics which lasts for 45 minutes.

On Wednesdays at 5:00 pm, Lachlan goes to orchestra which lasts for 45 minutes.

On Mondays, Lachlan goes swimming after his trumpet lesson and gets back to school at 5:30 pm.

On Fridays, before Scouts, Lachlan goes to his half hour guitar lesson. The lesson starts at 3:30 pm.

On Thursdays, Lachlan stays at school for art club which starts at 3:15 pm and ends at 4:15 pm.

On Tuesdays, Lachlan goes to computer club at 3:15 pm for an hour.

Draw your own timetable of things you do each week.

I can organise events and record them in a timetable

Calendar problems

Use this calendar to solve the problems below.

January						
S	M	T	W	T	F	S
						1
2	3	4	5	6	7	8
9	10	11	12	13	14	15
16	17	18	19	20	21	22
23	24	25	26	27	28	29
30	31					

February						
S	M	T	W	T	F	S
		1	2	3	4	5
6	7	8	9	10	11	12
13	14	15	16	17	18	19
20	21	22	23	24	25	26
27	28					

March						
S	M	T	W	T	F	S
		1	2	3	4	5
6	7	8	9	10	11	12
13	14	15	16	17	18	19
20	21	22	23	24	25	26
27	28	29	30	31		

April						
S	M	T	W	T	F	S
					1	2
3	4	5	6	7	8	9
10	11	12	13	14	15	16
17	18	19	20	21	22	23
24	25	26	27	28	29	30

May						
S	M	T	W	T	F	S
1	2	3	4	5	6	7
8	9	10	11	12	13	14
15	16	17	18	19	20	21
22	23	24	25	26	27	28
29	30	31				

June						
S	M	T	W	T	F	S
			1	2	3	4
5	6	7	8	9	10	11
12	13	14	15	16	17	18
19	20	21	22	23	24	25
26	27	28	29	30		

July						
S	M	T	W	T	F	S
					1	2
3	4	5	6	7	8	9
10	11	12	13	14	15	16
17	18	19	20	21	22	23
24	25	26	27	28	29	30
31						

August						
S	M	T	W	T	F	S
	1	2	3	4	5	6
7	8	9	10	11	12	13
14	15	16	17	18	19	20
21	22	23	24	25	26	27
28	29	30	31			

September						
S	M	T	W	T	F	S
				1	2	3
4	5	6	7	8	9	10
11	12	13	14	15	16	17
18	19	20	21	22	23	24
25	26	27	28	29	30	

October						
S	M	T	W	T	F	S
						1
2	3	4	5	6	7	8
9	10	11	12	13	14	15
16	17	18	19	20	21	22
23	24	25	26	27	28	29
30	31					

November						
S	M	T	W	T	F	S
		1	2	3	4	5
6	7	8	9	10	11	12
13	14	15	16	17	18	19
20	21	22	23	24	25	26
27	28	29	30			

December						
S	M	T	W	T	F	S
				1	2	3
4	5	6	7	8	9	10
11	12	13	14	15	16	17
18	19	20	21	22	23	24
25	26	27	28	29	30	31

How many months in the year shown:

1 start on a Monday
2 have a Friday 13th
3 have 5 Saturdays
4 end on a Wednesday
5 have 5 Thursdays, 5 Fridays and 5 Saturdays?
6 How often do consecutive months begin on the same day?

Compare this calendar with another year's and answer the same questions. Are there any patterns you notice?

I can solve calendar problems

Speed

Jo rides her motorbike at 40 miles an hour.
How far does she travel in:

1. 1 0 miles

1 $\frac{1}{4}$ hour

2 $\frac{1}{2}$ hour

3 $\frac{3}{4}$ hour

4 $1\frac{1}{2}$ hours?

Ken walks at 6 miles an hour.
How far does he walk in:

5 $\frac{1}{2}$ hour

6 $1\frac{1}{4}$ hours

7 2 hours

8 10 minutes?

Ginger drives her car at 60 miles an hour.
How far does she travel in:

9 10 minutes

10 5 minutes

11 1 minute

12 15 minutes?

True or false?

13 The distance you travel in a given amount
of time depends on your speed.

14 The slower you travel, the less time it will
take you to reach your destination.

15 The faster you travel, the further you will
go in a given amount of time.

I can solve simple speed problems

Speed

Mrs Jones usually drives at 40 miles an hour.
How long will it take her to drive:

1. $1\frac{1}{4}$ hour

1   10 miles

2   70 miles

3   90 miles

4   140 miles?

Kylie usually walks at 4 miles an hour.
How long will it take her to walk:

5   6 miles

6   8 miles

7   2 miles

8   14 miles?

A pilot flies a plane at 500 km per hour.
How long will it take to fly:

9   2000 km

10   250 km

11   4000 km

12   5500 km?

Harry must travel from Edinburgh to Inverness which is about 200 km.
How long will it take him to get there if he travels at:

13   20 km per hour

14   40 km per hour

13.   10 hours

15   50 km per hour

16   10 km per hour?

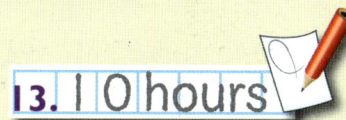

Which of Harry's speeds is nearest to 30 miles per hour?

Speed

1 Work with your partner to put these toy vehicles in order of speed.
(Hint: how long does each take to travel 1 m?)

Ben's tractor travelled
1 metre in 10 seconds.

Katy's plane travelled
20 metres in 10 seconds.

Marie's racing car travelled
3 metres in 15 seconds.

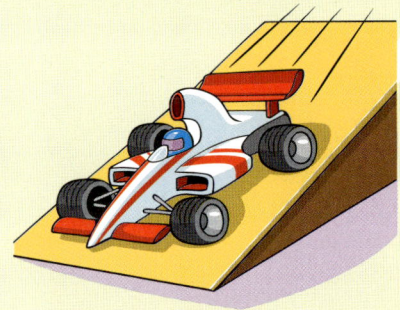

2. 8 0 kph

If 1·6 km = 1 mile, how many kilometres per hour is:

2 50 miles per hour   **3** 30 miles per hour

4 70 miles per hour   **5** 45 miles per hour?

I can solve simple speed problems

Time

| -7 | -6 | -5 | -4 | -3 | -2 | -1 | 0 | +1 | +2 | +3 | +4 | +5 | +6 | +7 | +8 | +9 |

Greenwich
Rome
Denver
New York
Singapore
All times are GMT.
Rio de Janeiro
Johannesburg

| 05:00 | 06:00 | 07:00 | 08:00 | 09:00 | 10:00 | 11:00 | 12:00 | 13:00 | 14:00 | 15:00 | 16:00 | 17:00 | 18:00 | 19:00 | 20:00 | 21:00 |

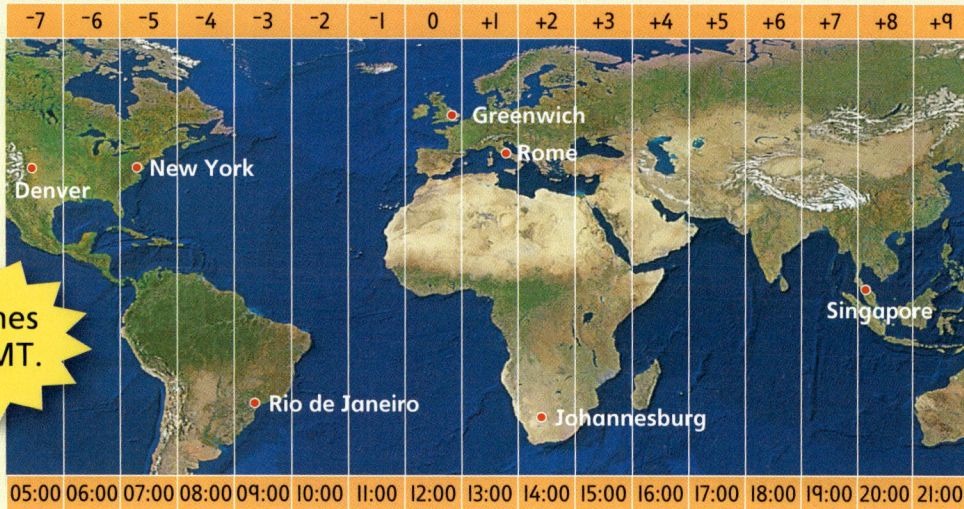

Write the time in each place when it is:

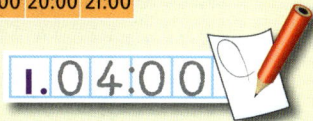

1. 02:00 in Greenwich
   ☐ in Johannesburg

2. 05:00 in Greenwich
   ☐ in Rome

3. 18:00 in Greenwich
   ☐ in Denver

4. 15:00 in Greenwich
   ☐ in New York

5. 19:00 in Greenwich
   ☐ in Singapore

6. 04:00 in Greenwich
   ☐ in Rio de Janeiro

7. 14:00 in Denver
   ☐ in Singapore

8. 01:00 in New York
   ☐ in Johannesburg

9. 21:00 in Rome
   ☐ in Rio de Janeiro

10. 11:00 in Johannesburg
    ☐ in Singapore

11. 22:00 in Singapore
    ☐ in New York

12. 06:00 in Denver
    ☐ in Rome.

Use an atlas to find places where the time would be the same on a 12 hour clock.

I can understand different time zones and find the times in different parts of the world

Time problems

In a relay race four children each run 200 m.

Here are their times:

Ali	43·2 seconds
Ba	51·8 seconds
Chrissie	48·7 seconds
Darren	46·6 seconds

1 Write the names of the children in order of speed, starting with the fastest.

2 How many seconds faster was Ali than Ba?

3 How many seconds faster was Darren than Ba?

4 What was the total time of all four runners?

5 Use a calculator to find the mean (average) time of the runners.

6 Another runner, Ed, can run 200 m in 47·9 seconds. Who could he replace in the team?

7 If Ed ran in the team in place of Ba, how much faster might they run the race altogether?

8 If the race started at 4:45 pm exactly, about what time did it finish?

9 How many tenths of a second quicker would Chrissie need to run to be as fast as Darren?

Fred runs a 1 km race at the same speed that Ba runs the 200 m race. With your partner, work out how long it takes Fred to run 1 km.

I can solve time problems

Estimating

Write the name of any items shown that, in real life:

1. car, ladder...

1   are longer or taller than a 30 cm ruler

2   are heavier than a 1 kg bag of sugar

3   hold more than a litre of water

4   are shorter than 10 cm

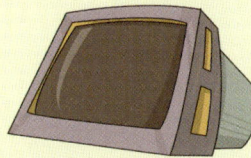

5   hold less than a litre

6   are lighter than 1 kg

7   are about 2 metres long

8   are shorter than a metre but longer than 30 cm

9   weigh less than a baby.

Choose two of the descriptions above. Write the names of some new items that match both descriptions.

Estimating

Write which you think is the best estimate.

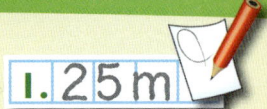

| 1.25 m |

1 The length of a tennis court.

| 250 m | 25 m | 25 cm |

2 The capacity of a kettle.

| 50 ml | 2 litres | 250 ml |

3 The weight of a box of matches.

| 1 kg | 600 g | 35 g |

4 The distance from Glasgow to London.

| 5000 km | 400 km | 3500 m |

5 The weight of a pound coin.

| 10 g | 900 g | 200 g |

6 The perimeter of a swimming pool.

| 500 cm | 2 km | 200 m |

7 The weight of a bucket of water.

| 600 g | 8 kg | 900 kg |

8 Write the names of six things you could measure. Write an estimate for each (either weight or length). Swap with your partner and see if they agree with your estimate.

I can estimate lengths, weights and capacities

Estimate

1 Estimate and then measure the length of each item below to the nearest half centimetre.

Draw a table and complete it to show your estimates and measurements.

Item	Estimate	Actual length
A	5 cm	..........cm
B		

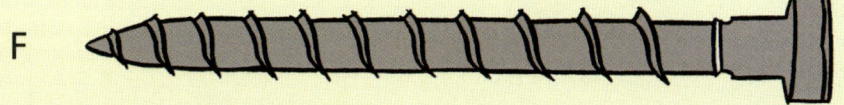

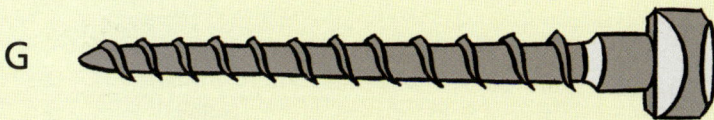

A

B

C

D

E

F

G

H

I

Write the name of some other items in your classroom that are about the same length as screw F.

Estimate

1 Find all the items shown below.

2 Estimate the lengths, widths or heights marked.

3 Now measure the lengths, widths or heights marked.

Item	Estimate	Actual length
Pencil	10·5 cm	..........cm
Paperclip		

4 Draw up a table to show your estimates and measurements.

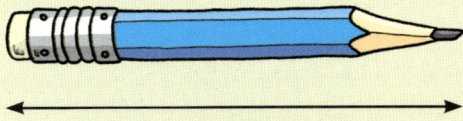

pencil

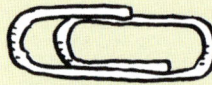

paperclip

glue stick

shoe

mug

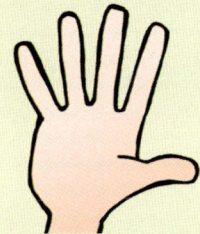

hand span

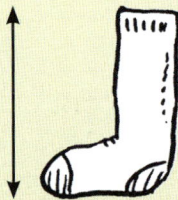

sock

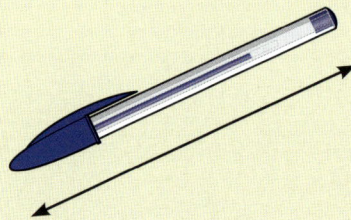

pen

book

Look at your estimates and measurements and find the difference in millimetres between them.

I can estimate and measure lengths

Estimating distance

Look at each picture. Estimate how far you think the person will travel in 10 minutes.

1.1 km

1

2

3

4

5

6

7

8

9

10 Compare your answers with your partner's. Try to reach an agreement about each one.

Imagine the length of your classroom in metres. How many centimetres is that? Inches? Yards? What other units can you convert your measurement to?

11 There are 36 inches in one yard.

An inch is about $2\frac{1}{2}$ cm.

Use this information to find out the approximate difference in length between a metre and a yard.

I can use units of length and convert between them

Weight

Write the most likely weight of each creature.

1. mouse 20 g

1

20 g 500 g 2 kg

2

3 kg 2 g 20 g

3

6 kg 20 kg 20 g

4

2 g 10 kg 100 kg

5

3 g 700 g 10 kg

6
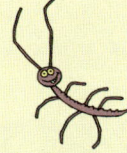
5 g 1 kg 2 kg

Take off your shoes! Feel their weight. Write an estimate in grams. Use scales to weigh them. How close was your estimate?

Write each weight in kilograms.
Use fractions instead of decimals.

7. $1250 g = 1\frac{1}{4} kg$

7

1250 g

8

1000 g

9

500 g

10

2500 g

11

2000 g

12

750 g

13
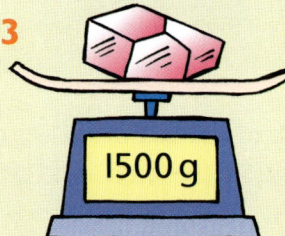
1500 g

14

2750 g

I can work with grams and kilograms

Grams and kilograms

Write each weight in kilograms.
Use decimals not fractions.

1. $650g = 0.65kg$

1

650 g

2

250 g

3

470 g

4
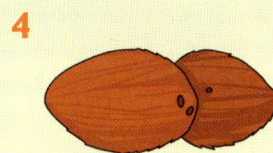
1010 g

5

1250 g

6

870 g

7

1650 g

8

720 g

Round the weight of each pet's
food to the nearest $\frac{1}{2}$ kilogram.

9. $800g \rightarrow 1kg$

9

800 g

10

450 g

11

900 g

12

600 g

13

200 g

14

700 g

15

300 g

16

100 g

Find $\frac{1}{8}$ kg in grams. Can you find other
fractions of a kilogram, e.g. $\frac{1}{5}$?

I can work with grams and kilograms

Kilograms and grams

Write the weight of each cake in kilograms.

1. $942g = 0.942 kg$

1

942 g

2

705 g

3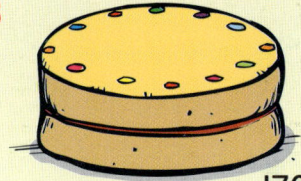

1704 g

4

1900 g

5

812 g

6

1010 g

7

1235 g

8

46 g

9

70 g

Write the weight of each book in grams.

10. $2030 g$

10

2·03 kg

11

3·104 kg

12

1·002 kg

13

4·05 kg

14

6·009 kg

15

0·85 kg

Weigh a book. Approximately how many of these will weigh 1 tonne? Discuss with your partner.

I can convert between units

Capacity

1 List the containers that hold less than
1 litre and write how much they contain.

1. (a) 2 5 0 m l ...

a 250 ml

b 1200 ml

c 1500 ml

d 500 ml

e 100 ml

f 1 l

g $\frac{3}{4}$ l

h 600 ml

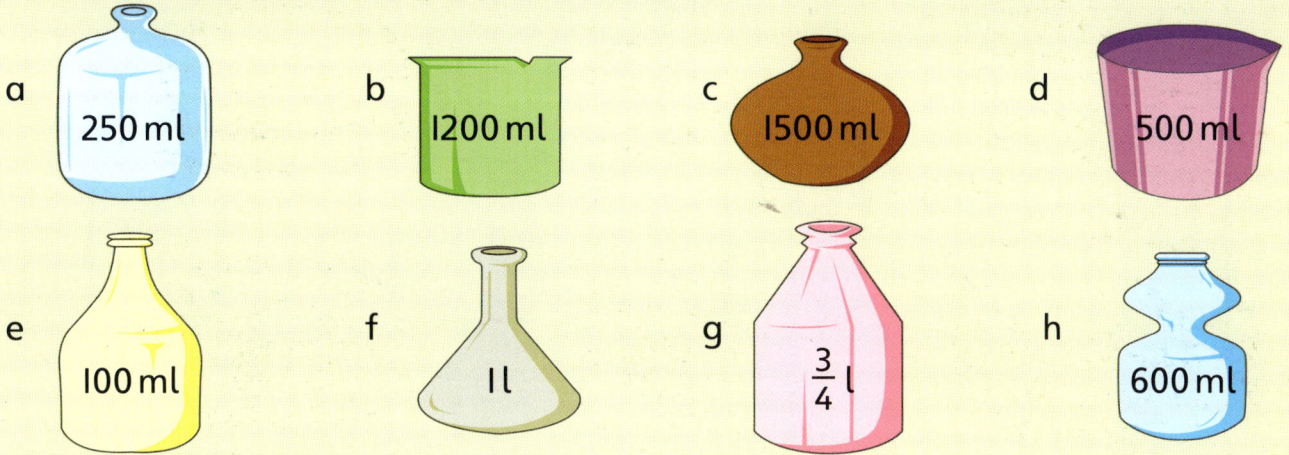

List the containers that hold less than half a litre.

How many mugs (containing 250 ml)
can be filled from a 2-pint bottle?

In each pair, identify the container that holds more.

2 450 ml $\frac{1}{2}$ l

3 $\frac{1}{4}$ l   200 ml

4 1 l   600 ml

5 $\frac{3}{4}$ l   700 ml

6 850 ml   1 l

7 $\frac{1}{2}$ l   550 ml

I can convert between millilitres and litres

Capacity

Write the number of millilitres.

1

$\frac{1}{2}$ l

2

$1\frac{1}{4}$ l

3

$\frac{1}{4}$ l

4

$\frac{3}{4}$ l

5

$1\frac{1}{2}$ l

6

$1\frac{3}{4}$ l

7

1 l

8

2 l

How many cups of 100 ml can be filled from a 5 l bucket? What about from a 10 l bucket?

9 Find pairs of containers that hold the same amount. Write the amount.

9. a and h 5 0 0 ml

a
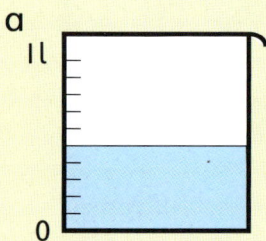

b
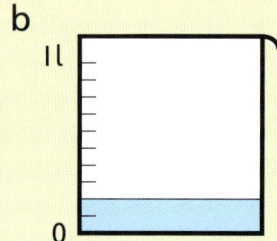

c

d
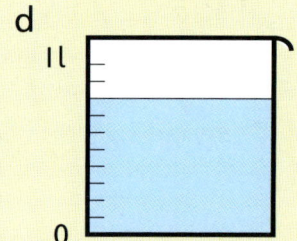

e
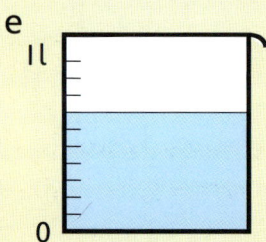

f
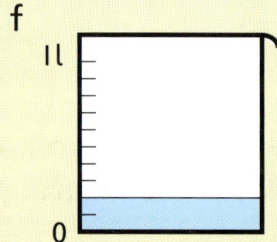

g
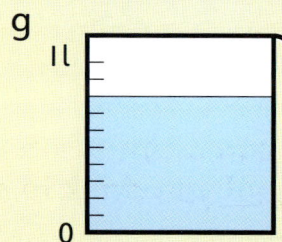

h
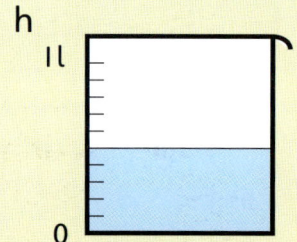

I can work with millilitres and litres

Capacity

Write the number of millilitres in each container.

1 $\frac{1}{2}$ litre

2 $\frac{3}{4}$ litre

3 $\frac{1}{10}$ litre

4 $\frac{1}{5}$ litre

5 $\frac{1}{4}$ litre

6 $\frac{1}{20}$ litre

7 Write these fractions of a litre in order, smallest to largest.

Read each scale. Write the amount of liquid in millilitres and in litres. Use fractions not decimals.

8. 5 0 0 ml = $\frac{1}{2}$ litre

8
1 litre

9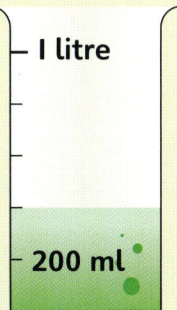
1 litre
200 ml

10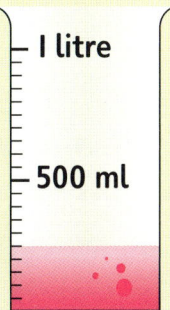
1 litre
500 ml

11
1 litre

12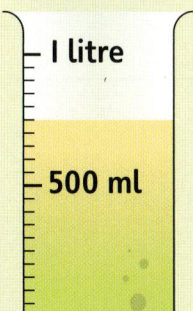
1 litre
500 ml

13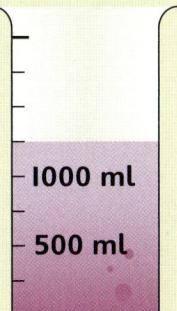
1000 ml
500 ml

14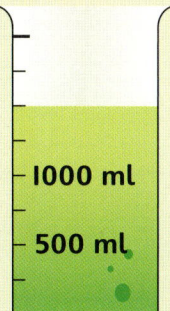
1000 ml
500 ml

15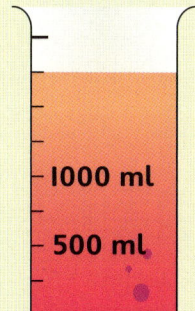
1000 ml
500 ml

A drinks can or mug can hold about 300 ml. Estimate how much liquid you drink in a day. How much in a week?

I can work with millilitres and litres

Litres and millilitres

Write the fraction of a litre in each jug.

1
100 ml

2
500 ml

3
250 ml

4
200 ml

5
750 ml

6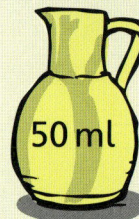
50 ml

1. $100 \text{ ml} = \dfrac{1}{10} \text{ l}$

Write each quantity of liquid using fractions of a litre.

7. $1.5 \text{ l} = 1\dfrac{1}{2} \text{ litres}$

7
1·5 l

8
1·75 l

9
1·25 l

10
1·1 l

11
2·25 l

12
3.75 l

Combine the amount in each pair of containers. Write the total in millilitres.

13
$\dfrac{1}{4}$ l $\dfrac{1}{2}$ l

14
$\dfrac{1}{10}$ l $\dfrac{3}{4}$ l

15
$\dfrac{1}{5}$ l $\dfrac{1}{10}$ l

16
$\dfrac{1}{4}$ l $\dfrac{1}{4}$ l

17
$\dfrac{1}{4}$ l $\dfrac{1}{4}$ l

18
$\dfrac{3}{10}$ l $\dfrac{1}{2}$ l

Two containers together hold $\dfrac{3}{4}$ l. One holds 300 ml more than the other. How much do they each hold?

I can convert between litres and millilitres including with fractions and decimals

Volume

10 litres is approximately 2·2 gallons

Write the approximate amount of fuel each person puts in their car, in gallons.

1. **8·8 gallons**

1

40 litres

2

100 litres

3

20 litres

4

60 litres

5

30 litres

6

5 litres

1 pint is approximately 570 ml

Each jug has a different amount of juice. Write the approximate amount in millilitres.

7. **285 ml**

7

$\frac{1}{2}$ pint

8

$2\frac{1}{2}$ pints

9

7 pints

10

10 pints

Find out how much blood you have in your body, in litres and in pints. Use the internet to help you.

I can convert between litres, pints and gallons

Area

Write the area of each rectangle.

1. Area = 15 cm²

1

2

3

4

5

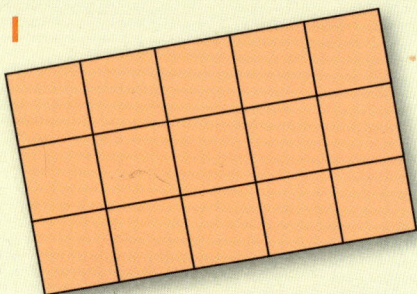

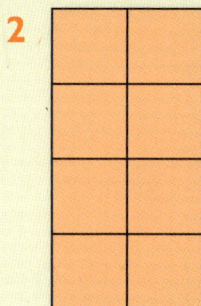

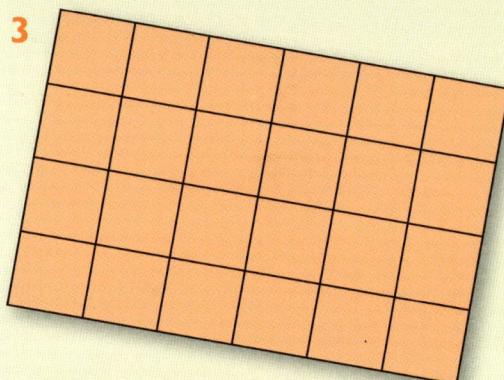

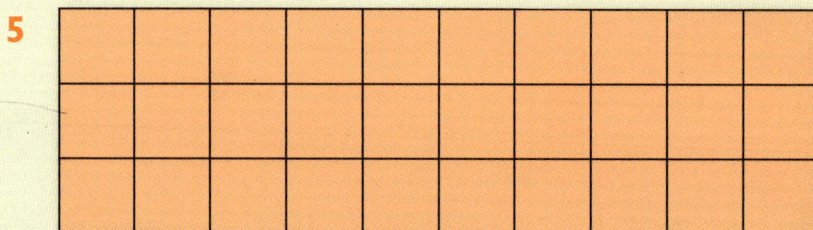

Measure the sides of these rectangles in centimetres.
Find the area of each in cm².

6

7

8

ULTIMATE STAR

Write a statement to explain to someone else how to find the area of a rectangle when you know its length and width.

I can find areas of rectangles

Perimeter

Find the perimeter of each poster.

1. P = 24 + 40 = 64 cm

1 12 cm / 20 cm

2 18 cm / 22 cm

3 30 cm / 45 cm

4 18 cm / 28 cm

5 42 cm / 20 cm

6 4·5 m / 3·7 m

7 2·3 m / 4·3 m

8 36 cm / 16 cm

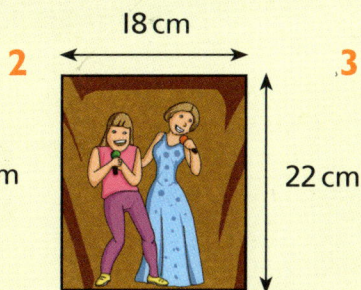

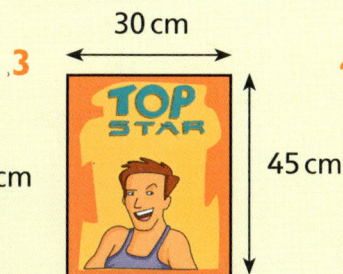

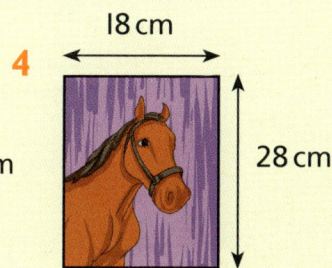

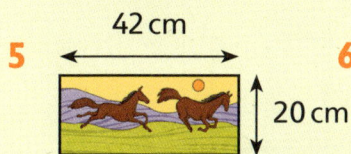

The perimeter of a rectangle is 36 cm.
Investigate what length sides the rectangle could have.

Write the perimeter of a:

9 rectangle measuring 7 cm by 6 cm

10 rectangle measuring 6·5 cm by 3·5 cm

11 square with a side of 8 cm

12 square with a side of 4·25 cm.

What is the perimeter of a square whose area is 25 cm²?

I can find perimeters of rectangles

Area

Tiny portraits are called 'miniatures'. Write the area of each miniature in square centimetres.

I. Area $= 8 \times 6 = 48 \, cm^2$

1
8 cm
6 cm

2
7 cm
9 cm

3
12 cm
8 cm

4
6 cm
3 cm

5
20 cm
11 cm

6
4 cm
10 cm

7
6 cm
8·5 cm

8
4·5 cm
7 cm

9
140 mm
60 mm

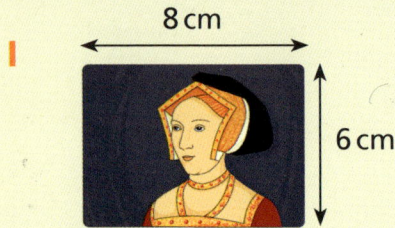

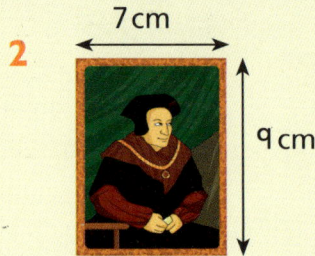

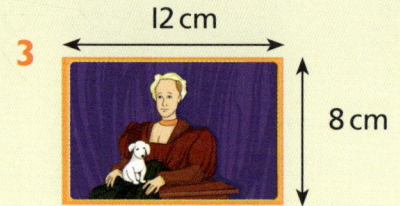

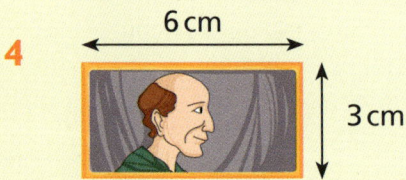

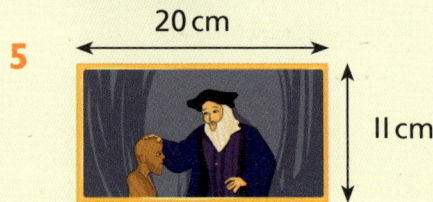

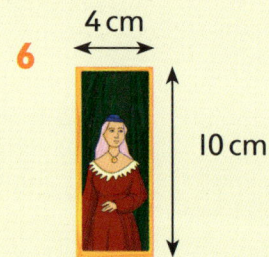

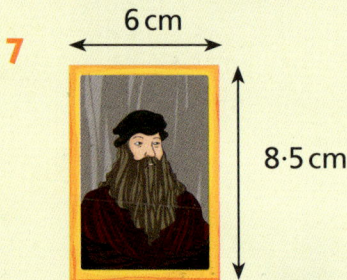

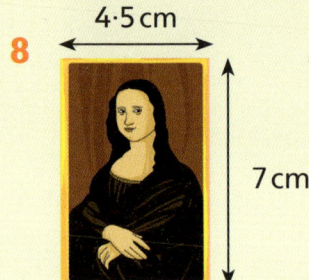

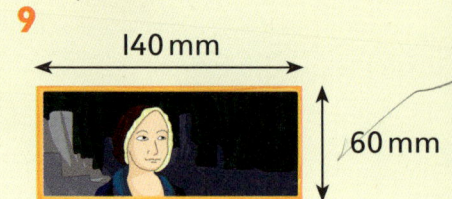

A rectangle has an area of 98 cm². Its length is double its width. How wide is it?

10 A garden has an area of 285 m², and it is 15 m wide. How long is the garden?

11 A square patio has an area of 81 m². How many centimetres long is the patio?

12 A carpet costs £4·50 per square metre. What is the cost of carpeting a room that measures 9 m by 7 m?

I can find areas of rectangles

Area

What units would you use to measure the area of:

1 this textbook page   **2** a postcard   **3** the floor

4 your toenail   **5** the playground   **6** Glasgow?

Think of something that has an area you could measure in two different units, such as cm² or m². Discuss it with your partner.

Write the area of these plots of land.

7. $13 \times 40 = 520 \, m^2$

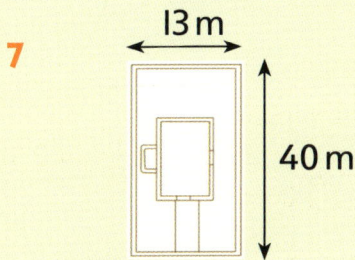

7 13 m, 40 m
28 Bush Street

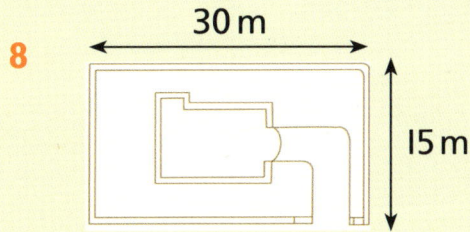

8 30 m, 15 m
35 Pine Avenue

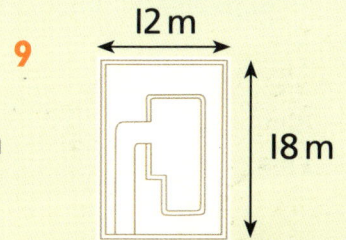

9 12 m, 18 m
101 Church Street

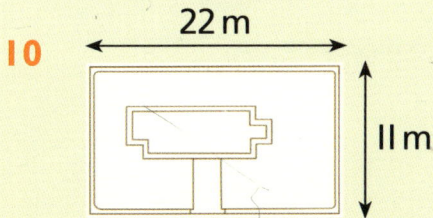

10 22 m, 11 m
48 Cherry Tree Road

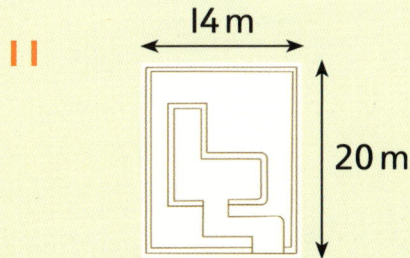

11 14 m, 20 m
6 Tulip Way

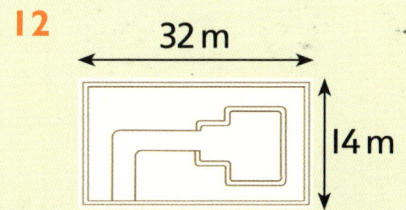

12 32 m, 14 m
17 Rabbit Lane

Draw a plan for a plot of land that is 20 m by 30 m, with a house and a garden. Find the area of the house and of the garden.

I can find areas of rectangles

Estimate

Write which you think is the best estimate.

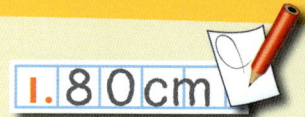

`1.80 cm`

1 The perimeter of a closed exercise book.

| 0·08 m | 8 m | 80 cm |

2 The area of a table mat.

| 600 cm² | 1 m² | 40 cm² |

3 The area of a piece of toast.

| 0·75 m² | 550 cm² | 150 cm² |

4 The perimeter of a stamp.

| 100 cm | 30 cm | 0·1 m |

5 The perimeter of a postcard.

| 0·2 m | 50 cm | 10 cm |

6 The area of a credit card.

| 40 cm² | 5 cm² | 500 cm² |

7 The area of a doormat.

| 12 m² | 28 cm² | 2·8 cm² |

8 Make up four estimates like this. Swap with your partner and see if they agree with your estimates.

I can estimate areas and perimeters

Perimeter

Write the perimeter of these regular polygons.

1   7 cm

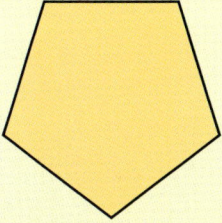

2   6·5 cm

3   4·5 cm

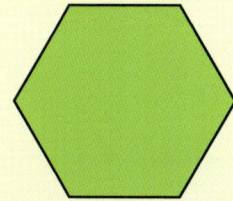

Write the length of a side of:

4   a regular octagon with a perimeter of 176 cm

5   an equilateral triangle with a perimeter of 48 mm

6   a regular decagon with a perimeter of 1·6 m.

A regular polygon has a perimeter of 60 cm. The sides are a whole number of centimetres. What might the shape be and how long would its sides be? Can you think of several different answers?

7   A rectangular picture has an area of 48 cm², and a perimeter of 28 cm. What size is the picture?

8   A square has a perimeter of 28 cm. What is its area?

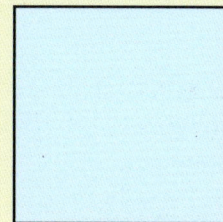

9   Measure the perimeter of this page to the nearest whole centimetre.

I can find perimeters of regular shapes

Perimeter

Write the perimeter of these shapes.

1. 14 cm

1

3 cm
4 cm

2

4.5 cm
2.6 cm

3

4.5 cm
11 cm

4

4 cm
7 cm
4 cm
12 cm

5

6 cm
5 cm
4 cm
6 cm
16 cm

6

10 cm
10 cm
12 cm
15 cm
15 cm
34 cm

7

1.04 m
35 cm
22 cm
1.2 m

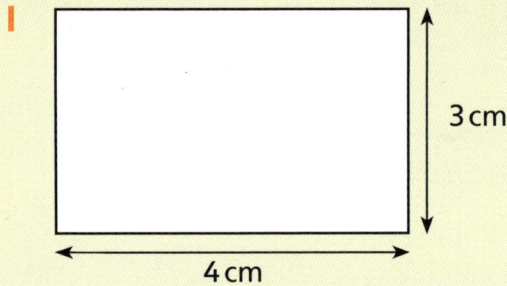

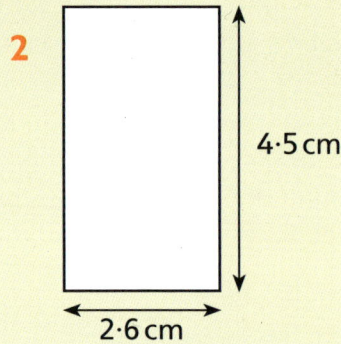

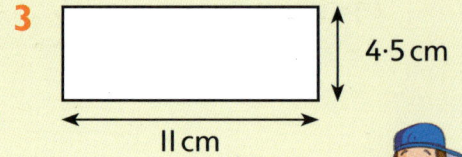

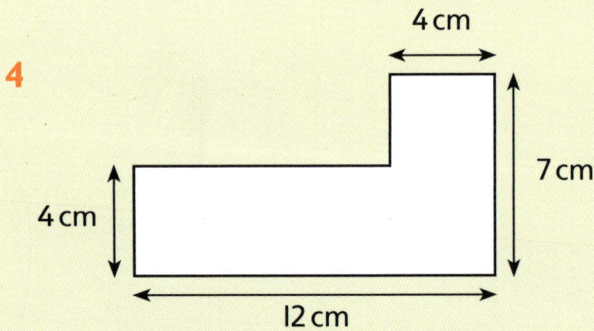

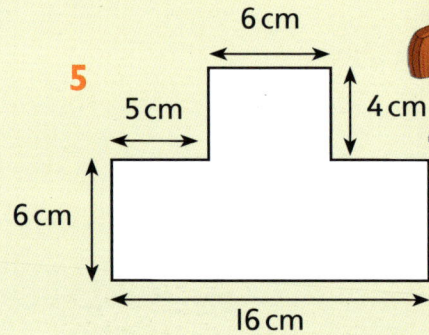

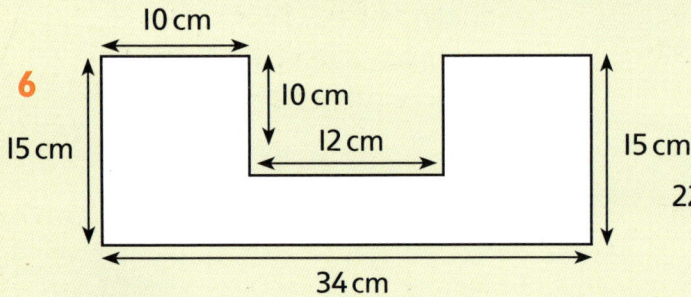

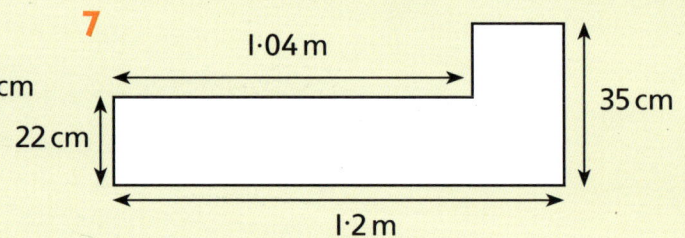

Use five squares of equal size.

Make different shapes by joining the squares edge to edge.

P = 10 units

How many different shapes can you make, and what are their perimeters?

P = 12 units

How many different perimeters can you find?

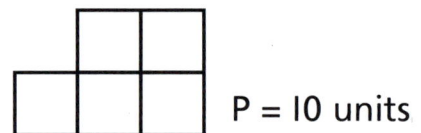

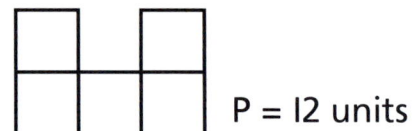

I can find the perimeters of shapes made from rectangles

Perimeter

1 Tim had a rectangular plot of allotment. One side was 12·5 m and the perimeter was 43 m. What was the length of the other side?

2 True or false? A rectangular garden with a perimeter of 50 m cannot have a side of 25 m.

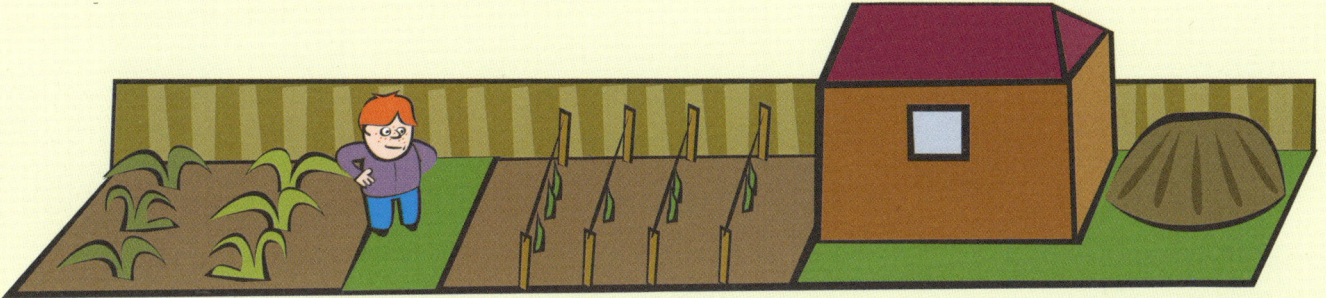

q
8
3
5
3
5
4
6

q
6
8
5

3 Find the perimeter of each shape. What do you notice about both of the red shapes? Both of the blue shapes?

Use this trick to find the lengths of the missing sides.

4. a = 3 units

4
2
a
c
7
4
b
P = 26 units

5
c
a
8
2
3
b
P = 24 units

6
c
4
6
3
a
b
P = 20 units

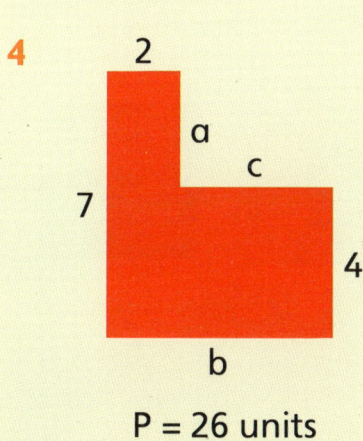

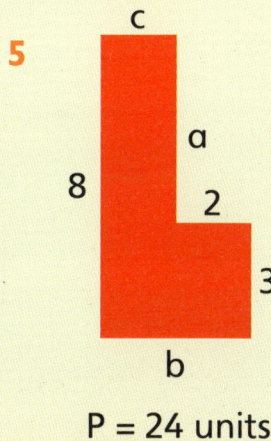

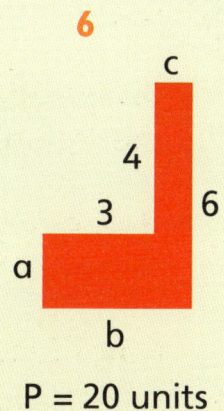

I can use patterns to help me find perimeters of shapes made from rectangles

Areas of rectangular shapes

Find the total shaded area.

1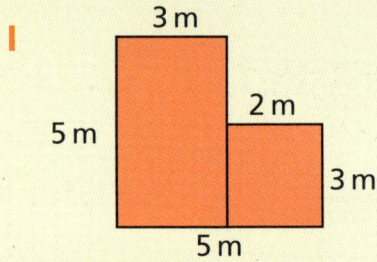

2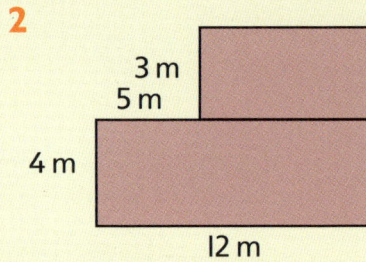

3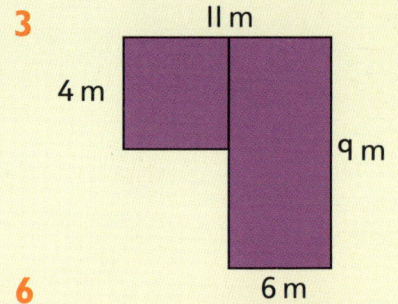

4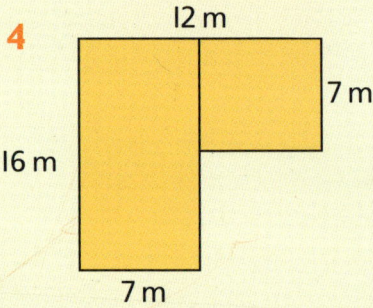

5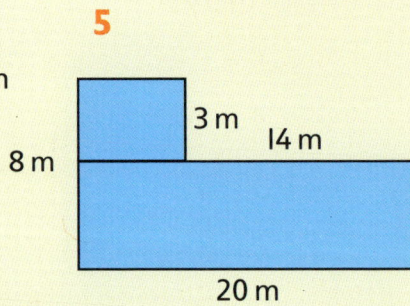

6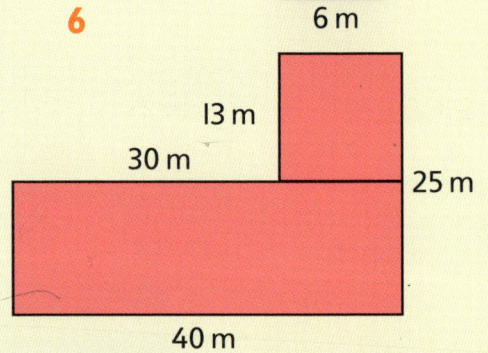

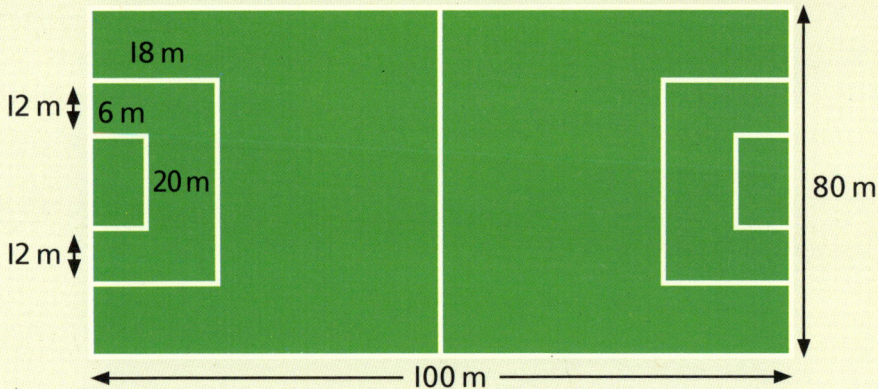

Find the area coloured red.

7. $6m \times 20m = 120m^2$

7

8

9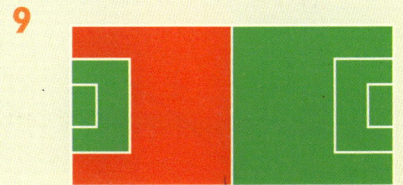

10

11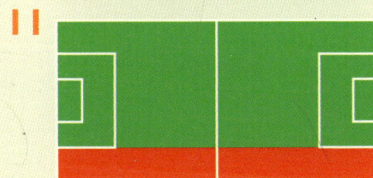

12

I can find the areas of shapes made from rectangles

Areas of rectangles

Calculate the area of the side of each bridge.

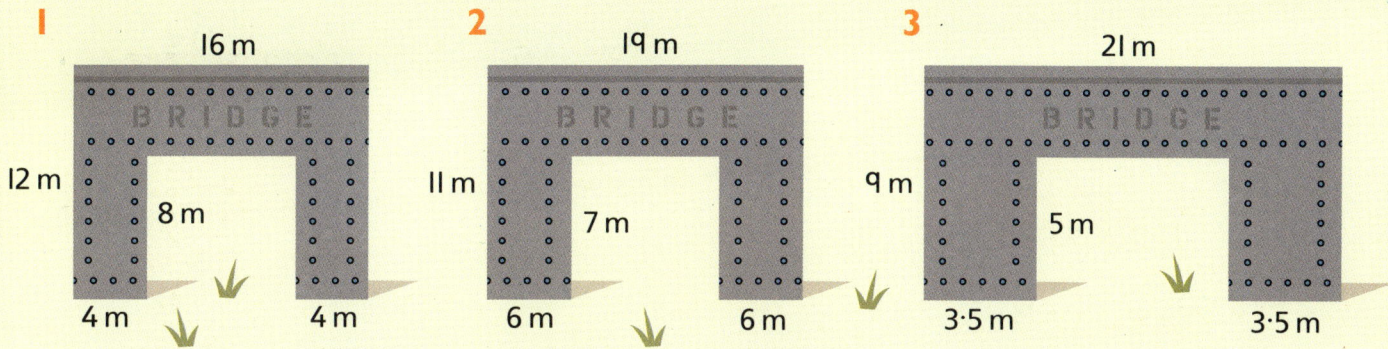

1
16 m · 12 m · 8 m · 4 m · 4 m

2
19 m · 11 m · 7 m · 6 m · 6 m

3
21 m · 9 m · 5 m · 3·5 m · 3·5 m

Find the area of each patio that can be walked on.

4
7 m · 3 m · 9 m · 4 m

5
14 m · 4 m · 4 m · 20 m · 4 m · 4 m

6
8·5 m · 9 m · 3·5 m · 2 m

Calculate the missing measurement of each rectangle. L stands for length, W for width and A for area.

7 L = 4 mm, W = 7 mm, A = ?

8 A = 120 cm², W = 10 cm, L = ?

9 A = 45 cm², L = 90 mm, W = ?

10 A = 27 cm², W = 4·5 cm, L = ?

Fiona draws rectangles on centimetre squared paper and finds their areas and perimeters. Write the length and width of each rectangle.

11 area = 12 cm², perimeter = 16 cm

12 area = 24 cm², perimeter = 20 cm

A = ▢ cm², P = ▢ cm. The number in each box is the same. Find the number.

I can find the areas of shapes made from rectangles

Areas of right-angled triangles

Calculate the area of the red triangle.

1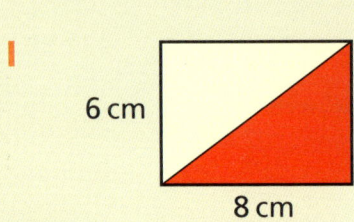
6 cm
8 cm

2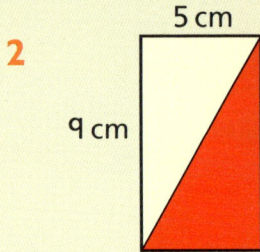
5 cm
9 cm

3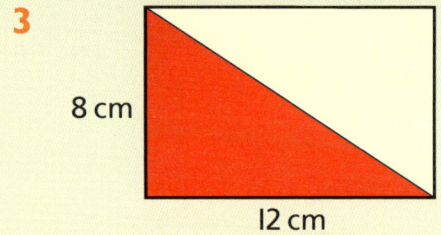
8 cm
12 cm

4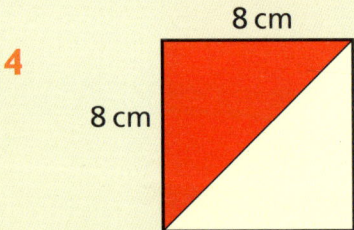
8 cm
8 cm

5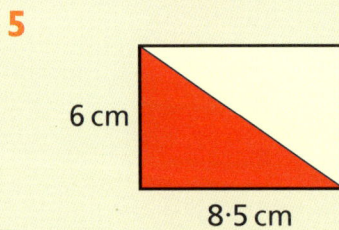
6 cm
8·5 cm

6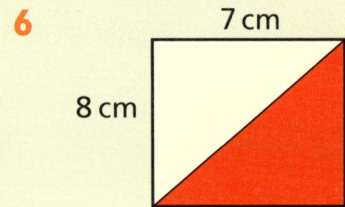
7 cm
8 cm

Calculate the area of this right-angled isosceles triangle.

4 cm   4 cm

Explore other triangles like this.

Calculate the area of each triangle.

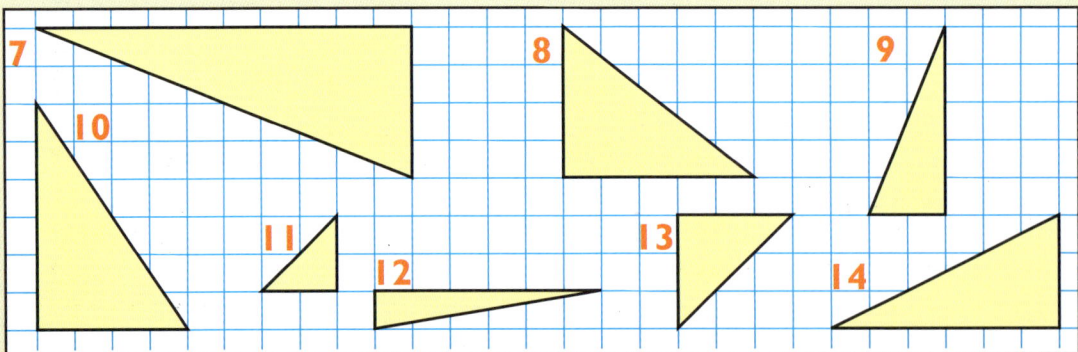

I can find areas of right-angled triangles

Areas of shapes

Lynda drew shapes on centimetre squared paper.
Find the areas of her shapes.

1. A = 2 cm²

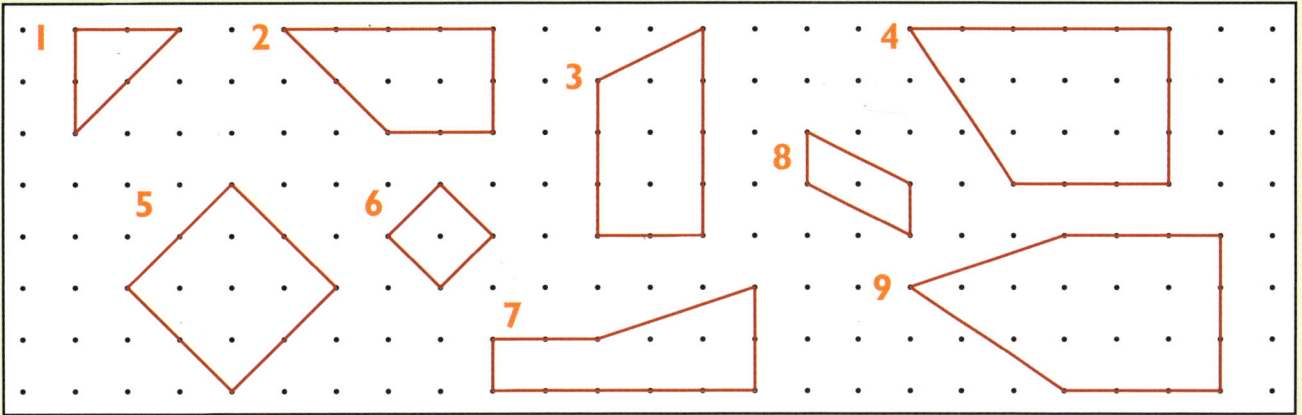

Calculate the length of the lettered sides.

10.(a)= 4 cm

10
10 cm
a
A = 20 cm²

11
8 cm
b
A = 24 cm²

12
7 cm
c
A = 31·5 cm²

13
5·5 cm
d
A = 22 cm²

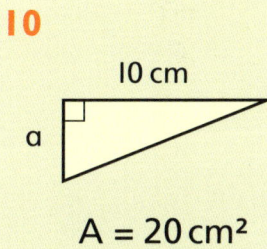

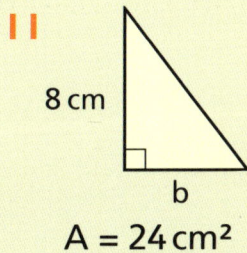

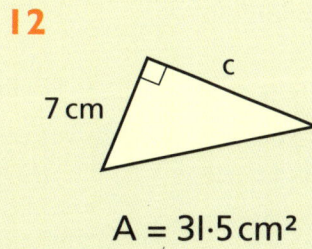

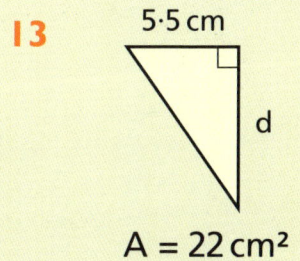

On a 3 × 3 dotty grid, create different polygons that have an area of 1 cm². Now try for shapes with areas $1\frac{1}{2}$ cm², 2 cm², $2\frac{1}{2}$ cm², ..., 4 cm². How many of each can you create?

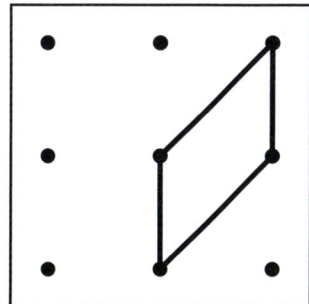

I can find the areas of shapes

Areas of non right-angled triangles

Calculate the areas of these non right-angled triangles by splitting them into two right-angled triangles.

1. $3 \times 9 = 27$
   $A = 13.5\,cm^2$
   $7 \times 9 = 63$
   $A = 31.5\,cm^2$
   Total area $= 13.5\,cm^2 + 31.5\,cm^2 = 45\,cm^2$

1 3 cm   7 cm   9 cm

2 5 cm   3 cm   6 cm

3 4 cm   7.5 cm   8 cm

4 8 cm   4 cm   4 cm

5 6.5 cm   12 cm   3 cm

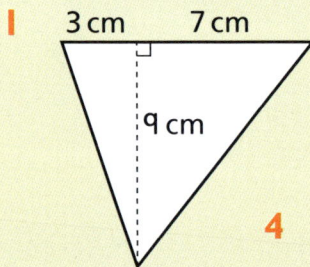

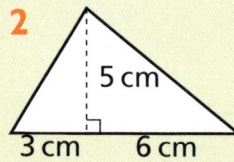

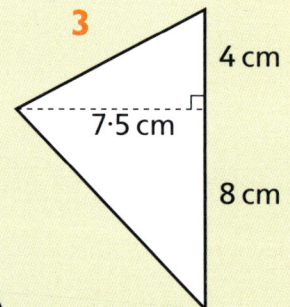

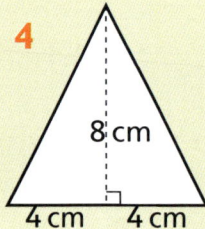

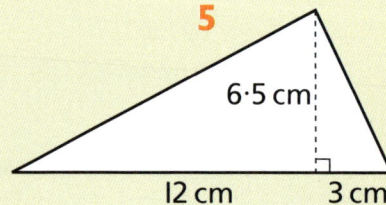

6 Ruth draws a rectangle that has a length of 12 cm and a width of 8 cm. She draws in both diagonals to create four triangles. Can you find the areas of the four triangles?

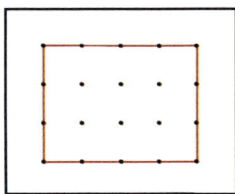

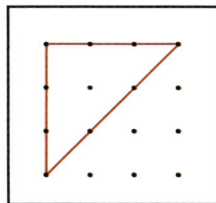

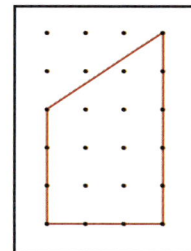

Draw some shapes of your own on squared dotty paper. Make sure you know their areas.

Give them to your partner and challenge them to work out the area of each one.

I can find the areas of shapes

Solids

You will need centimetre cubes in these four colours.
Make each model as shown in these pictures.

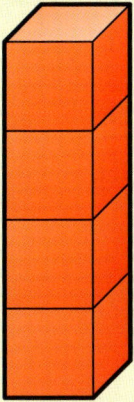

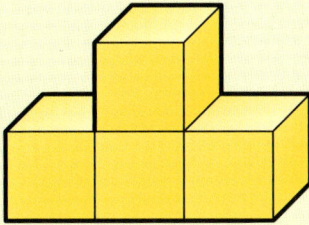

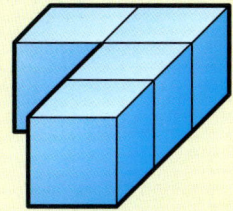

1. 4 cm^3

Write the volume of the:

1 red model   **2** yellow model   **3** green model   **4** blue model.

Each picture below shows a shape made from two of the models above.
The colours are not shown. For each picture, say which coloured models
are used and give the volume of each of these new shapes.

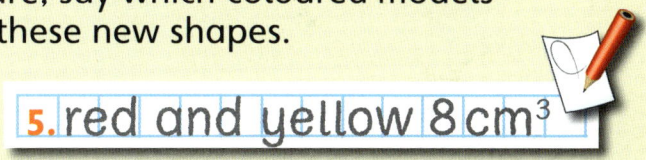

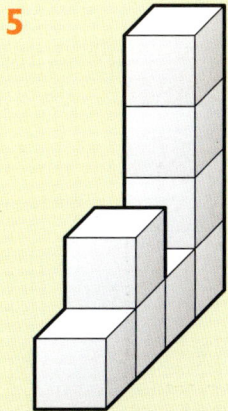

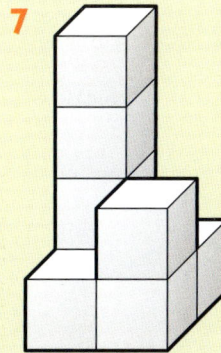

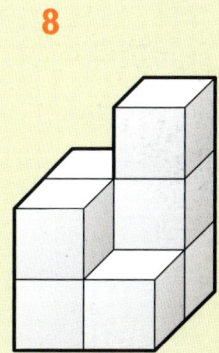

5. red and yellow 8 cm^3

5   **6**   **7**   **8**

9   Use all of the models to make this cuboid.
What is its volume?

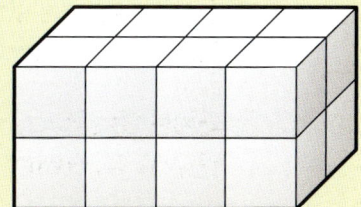

Surface area of cuboids

Calculate the surface area of each cuboid.

1. $(2 \times 9) + (2 \times 15) + (2 \times 15) = ...$

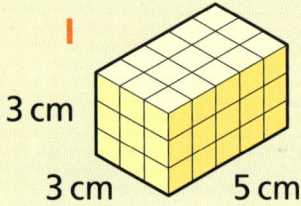

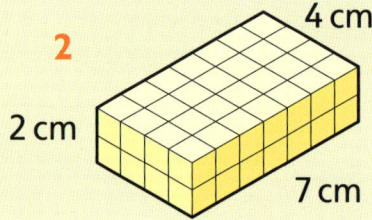

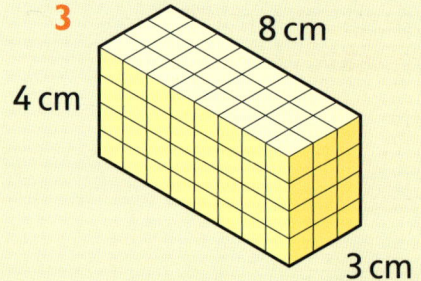

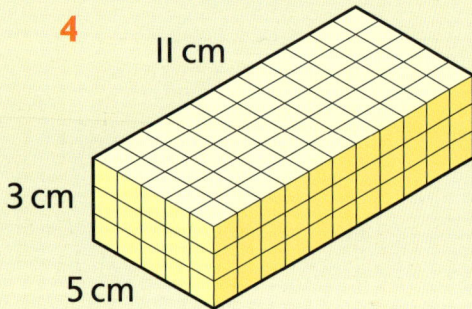

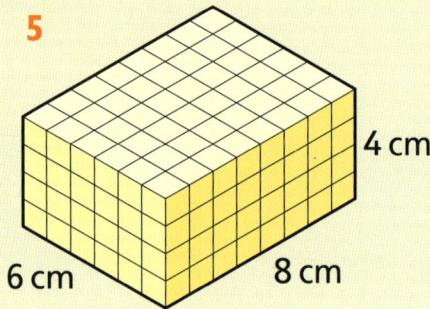

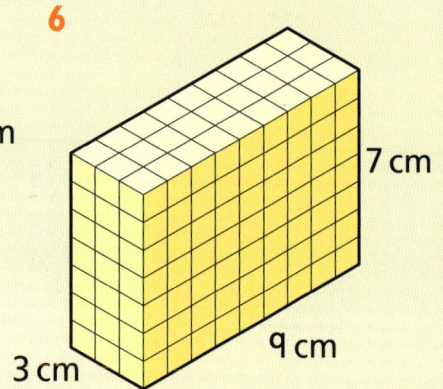

1
3 cm
3 cm
5 cm

2
4 cm
2 cm
7 cm

3
8 cm
4 cm
3 cm

4
11 cm
3 cm
5 cm

5
4 cm
6 cm
8 cm

6
7 cm
3 cm
9 cm

Use five cubes of the same size.

Make different models by joining them face to face.
Pretend the surfaces are flat.

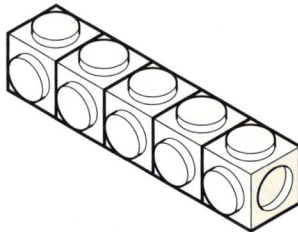

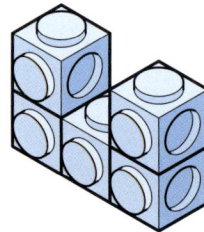

Investigate the surface areas of the models. Is it always the same?
If not, what are the smallest and largest surface areas?

Now try this using six cubes.

I can calculate surface areas of cuboids

Volume

Maxine made some solids from cubes.
Work out how many cubes are in each one.
Use your own cubes to help you if you want.

1. 22 cubes

1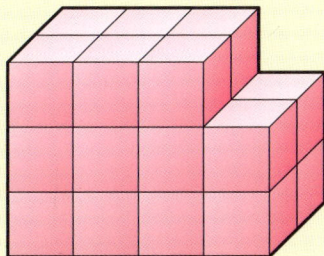

2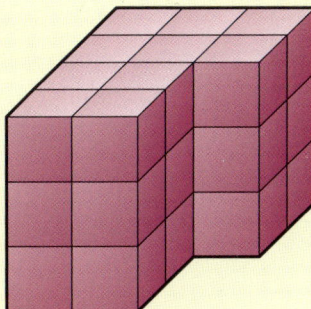

3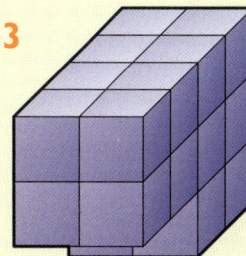

4

5

6

7

8

9

Make five different models with a volume of 30 cubes.

I can find the volumes of solids made from cuboids

Scale

These pictures show the dimensions of some doors in a town.
Draw each of the doors to scale, on squared paper, using the scale shown.

1

200 cm

60 cm

Use 1 cm to
represent every 10 cm

2

180 cm

80 cm

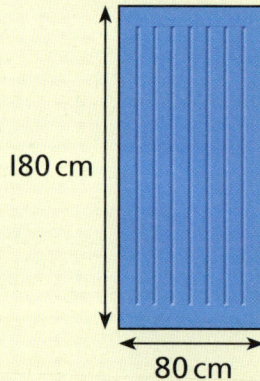

Use 1 cm to
represent every 20 cm

3

220 cm

165 cm

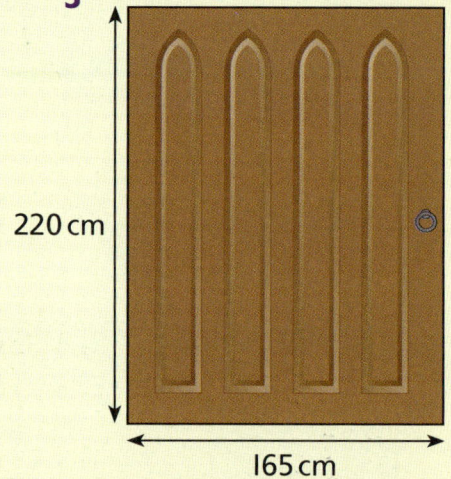

Use 1 cm to
represent every 11 cm

4

2 m

3 m

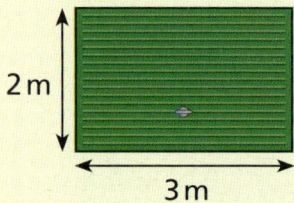

Use 4 cm to
represent every 1 m

5

FIRE

4 m

4·5 m

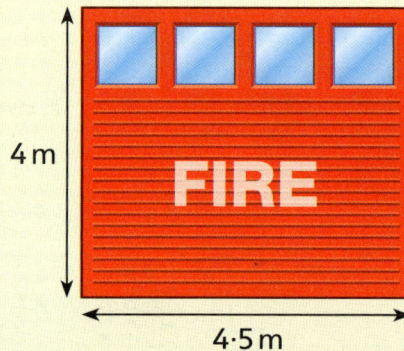

Use 2 cm to
represent every 1 m

6

5·5 m

2 m

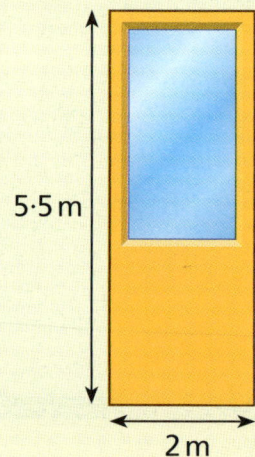

Use 1 cm to
represent every 0·5 m

I can calculate lengths using a scale and make simple scale drawings

Scale

This map has been drawn using this scale: 1 cm represents 50 miles.

1. Measure distances between pairs of towns on the map ('as the crow flies') and work out the distance it represents in reality.

1. London and Birmingham are about 2 cm apart. That is 100 miles in reality.

I can calculate lengths using a scale

Scale

These pictures show the 'elevations' (front views) of some buildings.
Draw each of them to scale, on squared paper, using the scales shown.
Include the doors and windows.

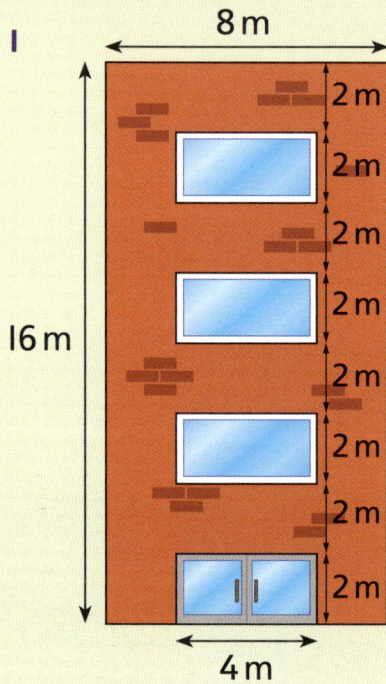

1

8 m
2 m
2 m
2 m
2 m
2 m
2 m
2 m
2 m
16 m
4 m

Use scale 1 cm represents 1 m

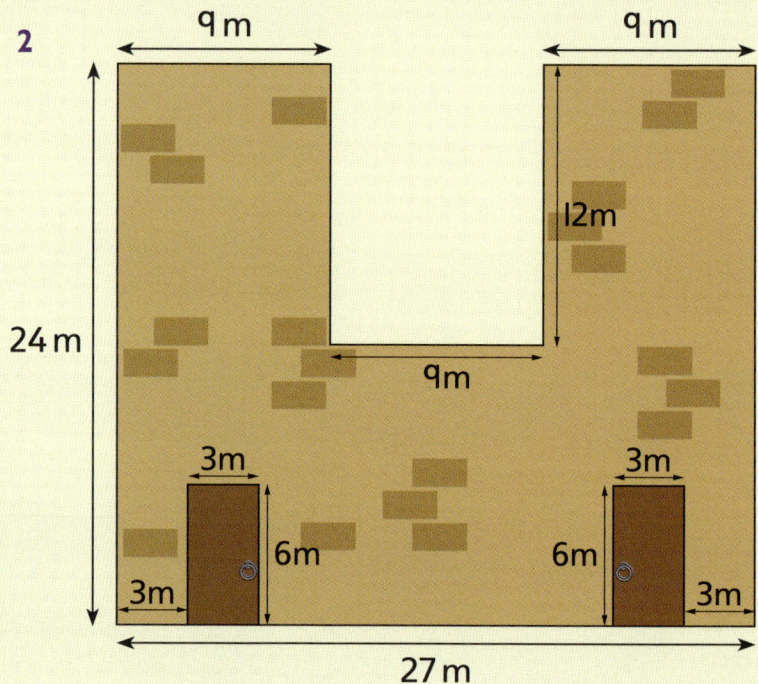

2

9 m
9 m
12m
24 m
9m
3m
3m
6m
6m
3m
3m
3m
27 m

Use scale 1 cm represents 2 m

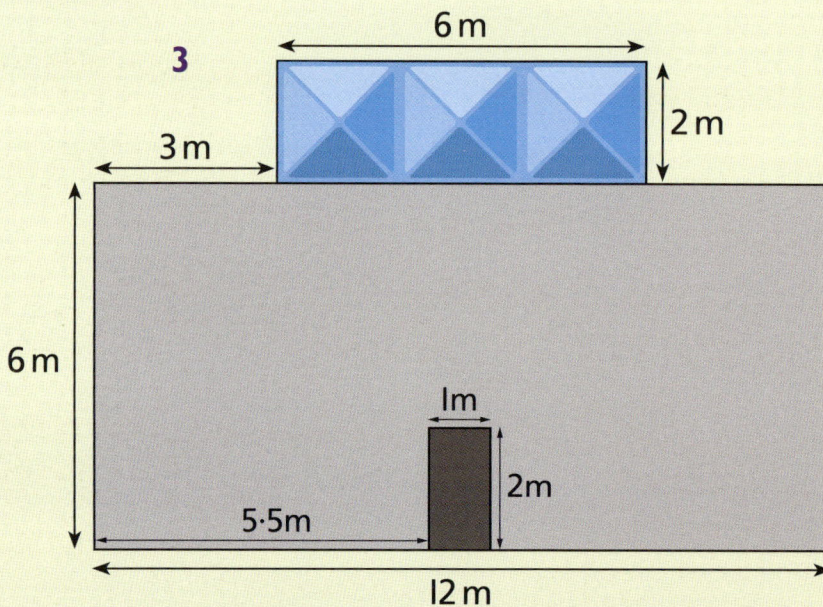

3

6 m
2 m
3 m
6 m
1m
2m
5·5m
12 m

Use scale 1 cm represents 0·5 m

Write the last scale in different ways, for example 2 cm represents 1 m.

I can calculate lengths using a scale and make simple scale drawings

Problems

1 A bottle contains 200 ml of shampoo. Beth uses 5 ml for each hair wash. How long will the bottle last if she washes her hair every day? How much longer would it last if she used 4 ml each day?

2 Dad fills a 100 l paddling pool with water. How many 1500 ml jugs will he need?

3 Amit uses 1500 ml of water to wash his dog. He does this once a week. How many litres does he use in 1 year?

4 How many 5 ml medicine spoonfuls can you get from a $1\frac{1}{4}$ l bottle of cough mixture?

If it takes 10 seconds for 1 l of water to run into a bath, how long does it take to fill a 160 l bath?

What is my perimeter?

5 I am a square. My area is 25 cm².

6 I am a rectangle. My length is twice my width. My area is 8 cm².

7 I am a regular pentagon. One of my sides is 6 cm long.

8 I am a regular hexagon. One of my sides is 7 cm long.

What is my area?

9 I am a rectangle. My perimeter is 16 cm. My length is three times my width.

10 I am a square. The number of square centimetres inside me is the same as the number of centimetres around my sides.

I can solve measurement problems

Problems

1 Sarah weighed 3·5 kg when she was born. She gained 125 g each week. How heavy was she in kilograms after 4 weeks? After 8 weeks?

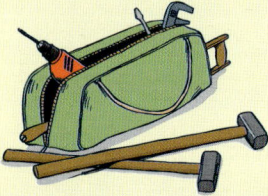

2 Craig's bag of tools weighs 9·4 kg. If he takes out two sledgehammers weighing 3400 g each, how heavy is his bag now?

3 Tara is going backpacking. Her rucksack weighs 26 050 g. The maximum amount it can weigh is 25 kg. How much weight must she lose?

Estimate how much a cat weighs. About how many cats weigh the same as you? Estimate how much an elephant weighs. About how many adults weigh the same as an elephant?

Calculate the thickness of each page in millimetres. There are 100 pages in each pile.

4. 4 c m = 4 0 mm
40 mm ÷ 1 0 0 = 0·4 mm

4 4 cm

5 7 cm

6 2 cm

7 5·4 cm

8 3·2 cm

9 6·1 cm

Take a dictionary and measure its thickness. Use a calculator to find the thickness of each page.

I can solve measurement problems

Measurement problems

Here is the nutritional information label from a can of baked beans.
GDA * stands for Guidance for Daily Amounts for adults.

Typical values	Per 100g	Per $\frac{1}{2}$ can	GDA *
Energy	73 calories	151 calories	2000 calories
Protein	4·9 g	10·0 g	45 g
Carbohydrate	12·9 g	26·7 g	230 g
(of which are sugars)	(5·0 g)	(10·4 g)	90 g
Fat	0·2 g	0·4 g	70 g
Fibre	3·8 g	7·9 g	24 g
Sodium	0·3 g	0·7 g	2·4 g
Salt equivalent	0·8 g	1·7 g	6 g

1   Devin eats a whole can of baked beans. How much fibre does it contain and what approximate fraction of his GDA of fibre is it?

2   Julia eats 400 g of baked beans. How many grams of sugar does she eat?

3   Sara eats $\frac{1}{2}$ can of baked beans. Approximately what fraction of her GDA of protein is this? Give the fraction in its simplest form.

4   Ben eats 300 g of baked beans. How many grams of sodium does he eat?

5   Sam eats some baked beans. He has one quarter of his GDA of sodium in this portion. How many grams is the portion of baked beans that he eats?

6   Clive eats 200 g of baked beans. How many grams of salt equivalent does it contain?

> Make up a problem of your own about the data in the table for your partner to solve.

We would like to say a special thanks to all of the children who entered our design a character competition, and congratulations to our winners!

WINNER

Character designed by Mhairi McGill, age 10
St Matthew's Primary School, Glasgow
Martin the Mathematical Fish

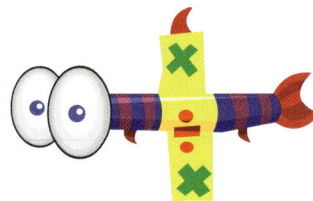

Interpretation of the winning design
by Volker Beisler
(professional illustrator)

Author Team:
Lynda Keith, Hilary Koll and Steve Mills

Published by Pearson Education Limited, Edinburgh Gate, Harlow, Essex, CM20 2JE.

www.pearsonschools.co.uk

Text © Pearson Education Limited 2011

Typeset by Debbie Oatley @ room9design
Illustrations © Harcourt Education Limited 2006-2007, Pearson Education Limited 2011
Illustrated by Matt Buckley, Seb Burnett, John Haslam, Anthony Rule, Debbie Oatley, Chris Winn, Piers Baker, Andrew Hennessey, Eric Smith, Gary Swift, Nigel Kitching, Mark Ruffle, Q2A Media, Jonathan Edwards, Stephen Elford, Sim Marriott, Andrew Painter, Fred Blunt, Emma Brownjohn, Tom Percival, Dale Sullivan, Tom Cole, Stephanie Strickland, Andy Hammond, Jackie Snider, Pet Gotohda, Annabel Tempest, Jim Peacock, Dave Williams
Cover design by Pearson Education Limited
Cover illustration Volker Beisler © Pearson Education Limited
Printed in the UK by Scotprint

The authors Lynda Keith, Hilary Koll and Steve Mills assert their moral right to be identified as the authors of this work.

First published 2011

15 14 13 12 11
10 9 8 7 6 5 4 3 2 1

British Library Cataloguing in Publication Data
A catalogue record for this book is available from the British Library

ISBN 978 0 4350 4795 5

Acknowledgements
Every effort has been made to contact copyright holders of material reproduced in this book.
Any omissions will be rectified in subsequent printings if notice is given to the publishers.